If I Were Going to Stay

If I Were Going to Stay

Jeanne Guillemin

Bauhan Publishing
PETERBOROUGH, NEW HAMPSHIRE
2023

Matthew and Jeanne, New York, 2010 — maxima amicitia

Printed and bound in New England, USA.
Bauhan Publishing, P.O. Box 117, Peterborough NH 03458
www.bauhanpublishing.com 603-567-4430
LCCN 2022945680 ISBN 978-087233-365-9

To Rob, John, Zoe, Amy,
Claire, Jake, Julia, Sam and Jesse

Untitled painting by Jeanne Guillemin-Meselson
(2011, oil on canvas, 11.5 x 8.5 inches)

Contents

Illustrations

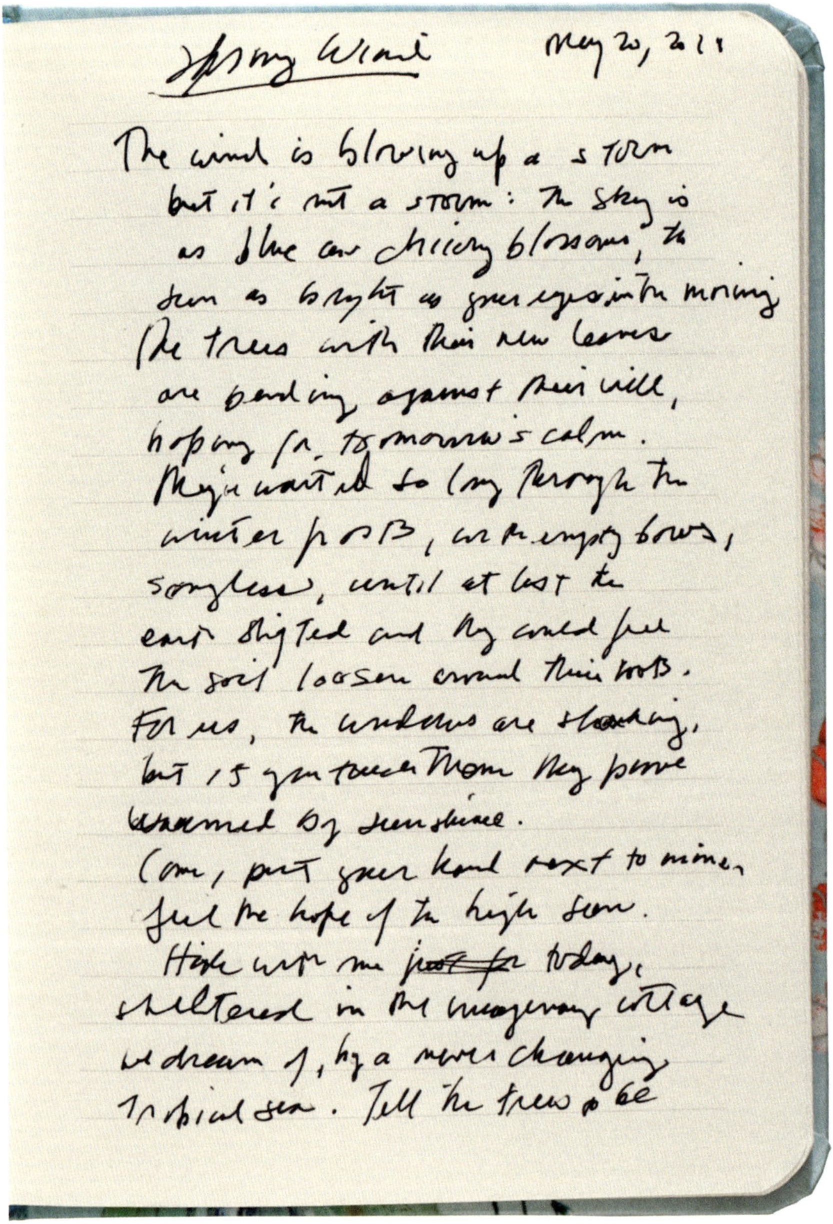

Spring Wind   May 20, 2011

The wind is blowing up a storm
but it's not a storm: the sky is
as blue as chicory blossoms, the
sun as bright as your eyes in the morning.
The trees with their new leaves
are bending against their will,
hoping for tomorrow's calm.
They've waited so long through the
winter frosts, with empty boughs,
songless, until at last the
earth shifted and they could feel
the soil loosen around their roots.
For us, the windows are shaking,
but if you touch them they prove
warmed by sunshine.
Come, put your hand next to mine,
feel the hope of the high sun.
Hide with me ~~just for~~ today,
sheltered in the imaginary cottage
we dream of, by a never changing
tropical sea. Tell the trees to be

First page of "Spring Wind" from one of Jeanne's notebooks

Foreword

Two months before Jeanne died of cancer, in 2019, she made a list of things to be done after her death. Along with instructions to give books, jewelry and paintings to family and friends, was the request: *Love poems — Gather them, investigate self-publishing, share with friends and family.*

I did not know of the list until after Jeanne died. No one, not even the four women in Jeanne's writing group of thirty years, knew that Jeanne wrote poetry.

The 78 poems in this book, remarkable for their emotional power, complex intelligence, and beauty of the words, are selected from 145 poems I found among Jeanne's papers and in her notebooks. The earliest of these is dated 1972, the latest 2016. Most are not dated. Some are typed, most are hand-written. Several, not included here, contain indecipherable words. The poems in this collection have been only lightly edited, for consistency of format. I have arranged them as best I could to reflect the course of Jeanne's life.

Jeanne wrote six published books and many published articles and book chapters. Why then were the poems kept secret? There is an answer in the poems. Some express love, profound or light-hearted, and uncommon wisdom. But others express the loneliness of love sought but not found. Some tell of happy childhood times with her beloved maternal grandmother Bessie, her adoring uncle Bill, and friends from school. But others tell of an autocratic father, an unloving older sister, a lonely first marriage and a terrifying divorce.

Despite the torment never entirely gone, Jeanne made a remarkable decision — to follow the path of love and kindness, so clear in these lines from "The Heel of August": ... *hoist up a skein of scars and love, hoist up the family bones heavy with anger, until they are luminous. Cure the blood with kindness, unrelenting gentleness ...*

Love and kindness, unrelenting gentleness — but also a wild heart, a free spirit. You can see it in the poems and photographs of Jeanne in this volume.

When Jeanne had just turned ten, her father abruptly moved the family from the friendly Brooklyn neighborhood where she had been born to Rutherford, New Jersey, a place of big houses, oblivious neighbors, and little of interest for a young girl. Alone much of the time, she read widely in books from the local public library. At age 12, after the family had moved to another New Jersey town, Jeanne entered a Dominican college preparatory school where she was taught by educated women who introduced their students to literature, history and art and took them to museums, opera and theatre in the City.

In 1962, against the will of her father and almost penniless, Jeanne went to Paris. There she attended classes at the École des Beaux-Arts and the Sorbonne, perfected her French and married Robert Guillemin, an American painter with whom, in 1964, she had twin boys, Rob and John. They left Paris for the US later that year.

Jeanne and Robert separated in 1975 and divorced in 1979, by which time she had earned a bachelor's degree from Harvard, a doctorate from Brandeis, and had become Professor of Sociology at Boston College. For Jeanne, teaching was an opportunity to explore with her students topics in anthropology and sociology relevant to their lives and families, producing a different, deeply researched syllabus nearly every year. As a single mother, she was just able to support herself and two sons and send them to a quality boarding school.

Jeanne and I met in the summer of 1981, at a conference in Aspen, Colorado. We became close but did not marry until December 1986. We lived in Cambridge, Massachusetts with summers in Woods Hole on Cape Cod, where Jeanne created a lively salon of humanists and scientists, lovingly guided the lives of her two young granddaughters, Rob's daughters Claire and Julia, and created an undisturbed space for her writing.

We traveled often, to a favorite Bahamian island, to Greece, to England and France, where we had friends and where Jeanne conducted research in the British and French National Archives on the Tokyo War Crimes Tribunal of 1946–1948, the subject of her last book *Hidden Atrocities*, and to Russia to investigate an outbreak of Anthrax, described in her book *Anthrax: The Investigation of a Deadly Outbreak*.

But why, although keeping her poems hidden while she lived, did Jeanne want them to be read after her death? Because she was a poet.

. . . I am a poet.
It's like God. I've denied it.
And life has denied it for me.
But nothing, absolutely
Nothing changes my soul or
Alters my sensibility.

Jeanne Guillemin, Cambridge, November 8, 1989

Matthew Meselson, Cambridge, August 2022

If I Were Going to Stay

Jeanne's First Communion, age seven
St. Vincent Ferrer Church, Brooklyn, New York

Brooklyn Botanic Garden
Spring

There I am, in a grey coat with
a white cotton collar, amazed.
Is this a graveyard? There are
wonderful flower beds that sink
under my patent leather shoes.
I should stay on the path.
My eyes are the height of my
mother's purse, patent leather too.
Everything is crackling.
Spring sharp. The tree
blossoms are sharp. The
tree bark is wet. I have
no idea what should
grow or die but all around
are flowers and my family.
Schrafft's chocolate will make
me sick by sunset.
Eat all you have been given.
Stay on the path.
All my clothes are new.
I am new.

Kiss

My Uncle Bill at Putnam Lake, when I was six
and wore a red wool tank suit, said "make
yourself a straight line," and his hand
under my back held me atop the
water. The first time he withdrew it,
I lost faith and collapsed. And so
again, straight line, enlarging faith, until
my whole body realized suspension between the
glowing summer air and the weight of water,
buoying wet sounds out of the air sounds,
cutting sun heat with lake cold.
My uncle laughed unheard to see his favorite
niece amazed and beatific, floating,
a more fierce vessel than anyone guessed,
become a kiss in search of a kiss.

Seeing as I Don't Like to Swim Alone

Life's choices, if you think of it,
may all come from the cautions that
one's parents brand into the nervous
system of the child, like the implication
that submersion into water over your
head or even at the tide's edge
with the whole complexity of the sea
staring back like an omnivore
is no fit venture in solitude,
that other heads should be bobbing
nearby or a hand grasped to
confront a wave that, to a child,
could seem a moving mountain,
a charging bull. Don't be alone,
comes the warning, when your
feet leave the pool's bottom or the wave
buoys you up weightless. Grab
for the hand.

Too Cold to Snow
Winter of 1952

It's a myth, what you said,
that the sky freezes
so hard the snow gets stuck above.
Proof is all around us.
Drifts and gray boulders at the
curb on 35th Street bury
the ashes of leaves.
Orange snowplows rumble past
the lady street guards at St. Vincent Ferrer's.
And from across the street
the boy I adore (I am nine)
whams a snowball at my woolen head.
It starbursts on my temple and I believe I hate him.
My shoes are soaked.
The snow is deep.
I am unprepared.

At Dinner

So what was the big idea?
I'm wondering at dinner
and will wonder all my life.
Was it that if we held our tongues,
stiffened our spines two inches from the chair back,
we could hold back the cold velocity of snow or stars?
Or let's, for sake of argument, make that frozen tears,
the real ones, implied in "I'll give you something to cry about."
Watch out, your dour look says
from the head of the table.
The world assaults. Nature betrays.
I see you are afraid and forgot about my shoes
turning to cardboard by the radiator.
Real laws are invisible until it snows.

The Heel of August

The heel of August
who can breathe this acid air?
You did. Angrier than anyone.
You, contusions, cuts, incisions,
incising the family bones,
soaking up the family blood,
the intelligent killing of me with
only eyes and acrimony.
All forgiven later? Not on your life.
All forgiven? You wasted to a vapor,
you had shrunk to glowing eyes. Never.
Split Adam's skull first, find
Golgotha, find his grave, over it hoist
up a skein of scars and love, hoist
up the family bones heavy with anger,
until they are luminous.
Cure the blood with kindness,
unrelenting gentleness, cry always
into the sky.

Anger

. . . with its unhappiness no one blamed you.
If it wasn't the jumps
it would have been you in pink toe shoes
checking your epaulement in the mirror
you slamming the door to your room
in anger that something was missing
that our parents slept on the other side of the wall
that the tree outside your window was so big
that the mirror kept giving back imperfect form
that you had to share anything,
certainly love.

The Invisible Father

The invisible father has moved to places I have never been.
He must be with the children who make him good.
He must not come too close or take shape.
That protoplasm is dangerous to him above all.
God bless his good works.

Cabbage Roses

They were our bedroom flowers
They were in my dreams
Renewed, repasted
But with the seams still showing.
How can I not be generous?

Parked Car

There must be times for everyone
just sitting in a parked car
thinking why did you start anything
when nothing is ever finished.
Why are packages forever being dropped
into mailboxes and delivered by trucks
and hardly one fact has been altered by words.
The women keep getting depressed.
Violence has a hurt and tired face, like
dented metal. I see its unblinking headlight
eyes and could swoon for fatality.
Loved in part, in parts, partly;
my breathing stops; the airless car
could snap, jump, roll over a hill,
take flight on wings of Mozart clarinets.
Love's body is broken and floating within
my head. How does anyone go on?

Becoming Like Everyone Else

Becoming like everyone else,
you sank beneath the ocean,
mirror eyes wide open, reflecting
yourself through opaque shafts of
light, shells, weeds.
Out of the sharp air into
soundlessness. Deaf, you
know the currents, but not me,
as I touch you dreaming,
and turn your copper stare to mine.

Zero Spring

I am suspended, transparent, unsleeping.
Until it passes my mind that
the narrow world he invented to which I was company
he has left, recommending spring in the abstract.
The door slams, shaking indoor and outdoor branches.
I mentioned the buds at Dumbarton Oaks
as particularly red and hard, a good sign,
but the comment was lost, ill-timed.
He will not sort the proddings of his spring
and will not set right my vision and truth.
The departure was civilly tormented, a ritual
of anger that moves like the leavings of thaw.
I am suspended, transparent, unsleeping.

July Night

Sweat is on the back of the baby's neck,
devils are rising up from the dirt of
the children's fingernails, unbreaking stillness
holds the trees. Even the two puppets
of memory, loneliness and sorrow, dangle
hollow-eyed in exhaustion.

I still ask where are you, though there is
hardly space for ribs or lungs to move,
though there is more blackness outside
this window than our eyes or mouths could hold.
Air hotness, body hotness, the same,
my skin waits for sleep with Laocoön restless wolves.

Colored balloons might rise in the morning,
if the roiling devils will kindly take prisoners,
if the trees can stop aching with immobility,
if the past gives in to the sheer weight of blood-black heat.
I ask again where are you, once so natural by me that
you left this night unnatural.

Broken in So Many Places

Life can be like that, suddenly
in a quiet space, if you can find it,
the fractures and fissures make themselves
known, having been silent, having held
their peace, as if you were intact,
merely shaken, not broken.
An intrusion of music, maybe a rapturous aria,
an adio by a doomed Butterfly or entombed Radames,
voices that are logarithms of fatal pain
as it is being absorbed, and
you feel every penetrating loss
that eluded the standard rituals, those crutches
of banality handed out at funerals or after
the shooting or car crash or the empty house,
when our speechless hearts break and break.

The Modern World

We're very cool except that
we die of longing every
night for perfect encircling
arms, passion and comfort,
an infinity of acceptance,
an infinity of control.

We dress together or rather
apart. It's futile to demand
what isn't there. A world
of raw hearts is no
less without purpose than
our hellos and bright goodbyes.

Like silkless silk
and milkless milk
we're growing used
to loveless love.

Cruiser

If I am a boat, you will watch me
sail out of this harbor with grace
under the pressure of bluest day
against the pressure of darkest waters.

We abandon each other constantly,
promising with our hands to save,
with our eyes to understand, with
our thoughts to rescue, hints of
salvation and new formulas for faith.

I have watched you from the land.
I never leave and traced your course
on the horizon: cruiser, your
harbors are the Corinths you create.

November 2, 1976

Genocide 1976

Twelve books behind me on the shelf,
each full of dust and death.
Regimented rag-tag like the old guard,
stragglers from Zulu Wars,
toppled from horses on the plains
armed with the rusted guns
of old brutalities.

And in my hands in a new
and blacker binding:
Worse destruction, unnatural funerals
the order of madness, impossible innocence
delivered to sanity by
princely reason.

A ray of light? You are.

Wareham

The fieldstone foundation of the main house is nearly buried.
Who remembers the hurricane of '38?
This rectangle of stone moans, breathes, "I am open."
What mattered may never matter again.
The new house went up deeper in the cove.
Three cedars bank the stone wall against the bay.
Still nothing stays the same. Every year
the water breaks through the sand in a different way and
floods the flatland.
Now this room, six windows to the water,
is filling with sand and light.

In 1974 Tommy the harlequin baby came here
and in one month his right side grew almost as muscular
as his left, his heart pulled his weaker half along.
By now he must be almost right or as right as any of us.

In 1977 the beautiful white-haired anthropologist
keened out the Sioux women's Song of the Sun
and raised the hair on our civilized spines.
All six of us full of vodka, I drove my convertible blind around
the shoals of country roads
and Rosalie, still self-transported,
sang Gretchen's song into the trees.
The black cedars come suspended through the windows:
We are words. The words change this room.
The hundreds of homecomings and departures
continually shatter what this place is.
The long heavy table Mr. Hennicott made
pushes against the sea light and against the elbows, wrists, and voices.
I mean here, here.
We had no home once but here.

Green on Snow

If at the last minute the ocean air
had not met some following of clouds
and made snow, late winter snow,
over the alyssum, the budding peonies,
but left us the continuity of spring
to summer. And if the leaves
had not caught the weight
of snow, bent and broken the trees,
wires would not have arced and
smoked on the front stairs.
We could have seen a life run
straight, a natural evolution in the
jumps and starts of days and distance.
I called but the wires were down.
The phone rang somewhere but did not
ring at all. Sound leaped and
I thought I saw you again in the
melting woods, an eye cast to me, a hand raised.

May 11, 1977

Kevin

We sat and drank to each other,
suspended somewhere in late July,
our urgency belied by café shade,
trapped and sheltered at leisure.

Would-be tourists are sprawled
throughout the airport lounges of the West.
We have not moved from under lemon umbrellas,
from the white metal table that slightly rocks.

You might move your brown arm
through the near glare of the sun
and disturb the iridescent air to waves
outside this circle of near recollection.

Or I can catch on my sleeve and back
the secondary rotations of leaves,
patterned movements of branch and air
in partial forms fixed in the weight of heat.

Somewhere else Tropical Storm Amelia has risen
and died. We drink each other's tears
under the possibility of clouds scattered
from Cape Hatteras to Mt. Desert.

In trying to remember how well
we knew each other, when presence
signaled the end of boundaries, all
by eye, by mouth, by hand erased.

Tickets and Trains at Trenton

When the train moves, I cannot write.
The reduced fare ticket is void at eleven; the train is
due at 11:04. When the train moves,
I can barely walk. Last night, I just
wanted to be transported home, to my own room,
the twin ivy plants, out of your schedule's
imperatives to my day's needs, the light shifting
through the shutters at eight, one, four
o'clock. I heard you restless turn, I turned in pain,
punished and bereft.
Headlines: though exhausted the one more
loving strikes a blow for the imagination of kindness.
The teeth are rattling in my head from the effort:
I posit you care for me
in the face of negligible evidence.

So go to Mexico; I have made an altar
of lavender buds, a Pontormo angel's face,
and my phone. So go to L.A. for supper.
I've plans to wax the furniture, write a friend,
avoid unnecessary conflicts with fellow workers
and go to Symphony. Punished and bereft.

October 6, 1978

Separation

The truck withheld within it
a two-month coolness.
We had a style of being together
which in bearing the burden of
intimacy proved as awkward
as an adolescent. Shy to sit
or lie down, still more shy in
standing. Talk about things,
talk about nothing.
My hands are straining to
remember what you will not tell.
The curve of your hip to your thigh,
the muscled arch of your neck, and
what your skin reveals as response
to the woman you've stayed with,
like a mastiff you've brought along
to guard me off, a chemical
statement of fidelity and fear.

March 7, 1979

The Carmelites in Brooklyn

Hear the cloistered Carmelites sing
sweet eternity up from the high-walled
garden on Bedford Avenue, invisible women
celestially assured that atonement
in silent prayer will create all their days till death.

Whose singing I heard leap up to Bessie's kitchen
window at the time of cooking great heavy meals
for her seven children and their children.
We all thought that our sheer numbers
guaranteed the ritual punctuation
of Thanksgiving, Christmas, Easter.
We did not understand that families
die or are dismembered.

My own loves dispersed, with no holiday plans
this year, I hear those vesper voices again
rising over the trees of heaven, coming like
salvation's dawn, chanting their only
audible ecstasy, "Forever, oh, forever
springs from our bodies and never, never
from yours. Amen."

The Sweet Dying Woman

The sweet dying woman with whom I shared a cab,
she came from National to Longworth,
from a wheelchair the cabbie thought
he would have to pack in the trunk.

Her nails were perfectly manicured.
I saw them as her hands took hold of the sides of the car door
opening, hoisting herself, so little of herself,
into espadrilles, onto the sidewalk and then,
with a painful shuffle to the door,
to the policeman, asking for change and back again.
So sweet, with swollen ankles,
with shoulder blades
sharp through her jacket.

I got out and handed her a shopping bag full of
manila folders and envelopes. Is it that there are
so many women in Washington that more women seem
to die? Or do they really die younger here,
with a civil sweetness, with fine hands?

April 18, 1979

Sand Games

Let us make a castle house of ample rooms,
filled with furniture and the cries of
children, a Christmas tree that stands
until February, infant eyelashes so long
they catch the tinsel, a cat asleep atop
the upright piano. On the porch returning friends
unhurried in their conversations through long
July evenings clink their glasses and
eat until they leave or tumble upstairs
into Victorian amplitude to sleep.

Frightened for nameless causes,
unforgiving, through the tinsel tears
of children, we fought to lock one room
and then another. Moats were dug, turrets
collapsed, halls swelled with sadness, the heart
chambers of the house rushed with anger. The castle
tilted ignorant and astonished. Plates, sofas, sheets
scattered. The old doors blew open as our lives'
things tumbled like us to curbside and other lives.

Divorce

It's called Breakage.
And begins with "Oh, no!"
All the things from the Newton
house dumped and scavenged violently in
the street. Oh, no. Mine!
Wait. My portrait was torn
from the gold wood frame
and the frame taken away. I left
me, my smiling bright face in the
trash with everything and he took
the rest in rented truck.
Broken! Broken! Broken!
Who says there was no
breakage? Nothing hurtful?

Snow

I will come to love snow
as texture against brick,
as motion of flowers,
as water in waves,
for what it appears to be
and not for the cold it signals.

Brighton, November 1979

In My Father's Eyes

In my father's eyes I saw
the wit of my son, the
intelligence that danced
complex in perfect
form; and in your eyes,
for which I could not but
love you, the same dance
but broken, burnt, a
dying wild, sobbing and
petulant; a bright and
wild stumbling; I could
not hold you as I held
my son or guided
my father's steps.

Oak and Iron

I have not understood the different shapes of love,
the signals sent shyly across a dining table,
special offers lost like sighs, or concert programs
he kept and I never thought to.
Philosophically I mourned the lack of loving in the world.

And Kevin (long after we were lovers and as we
sat and drank café wine) said with surprise
"But we did!" Had I missed that old quality of affection,
in one man extraordinary patience, in another
books and more books, in another the dignity of state occasions?

What vessel have I been sailing on, that I feel only
the single continuous roll of an ocean I cannot see,
an ocean I breathe, a vessel of oak and iron history.

Bird and Fish

For all these self-inflicted wounds
I tend and randomly renew
in paradox of flight and fall.
For all the restless sad distance
you must impose and navigate
in the ocean of memory.
Sometimes I've caught you fast,
beached in shallows of now
hosted by coastal topology
to a tranquil, azure integer.
And you called the sea bird,
stunned my bright eye with yours,
in alchemy turned flight to dance,
I blessed the trembling, blessing you.

July 21, 1982

The Red Cat

The red cat called at my window.
It didn't seem a bad idea,
the snow being hard as stone,
to claim beneficence,
being alone.

An alley cat of grace,
but skittish on his cold pink paws,
he leapt a crooked path,
windowsill to kitchen,
kitchen to bath.

If your wife should call you again,
insist you take the kids tonight,
would firmness queer the game,
abandon and cry out?
Leave it the same?

The orange beast with pointed teeth
lies restless on my desk,
disturbs without a care
my work's serene intent,
the heart I'd dare.

July 15, 1983

Landscape

I caught you as you fell, a torso of ice, grief-taster,
wanderer in the circle of an eye, on the moon-struck plane
by the sea without light, in the full season of desolation.

We were weightless in the silver night, so blessed in isolation,
so damned in the privacy of our flight.

October 1983

What Could Be Better?

What could be better or
brighter than a July
night on Newbury Street,
our kisses as chill as our
white wine in the street café.
No prospects, only you and me,
no ties to bind,
never-ending night.

Persuasion

When I call rejoice and rise up,
you wild Isaiahs, will
these isolated sensibilities
turn, culminate? I have
cast off the anguish that
tore, made me a red flower,
the strength of my children's
virtue renewed: I touch it
and am saved. This living light is
everywhere, on the salt-bitter
sea, on the honey clover, in
all journeys comes the radiance.
Are you willing?
Have you waited for the day?
Parthenia!
The hyacinthine egg is burst!
We are at last the colors of love
and we shall sing together.

November 11, 1983

Jeanne and Matthew, Hydra, 2016

New Hampshire

I could wake this whole house
with cries of three-in-the-morning strife,
to your sleeping children and mine,
that you turned around and turned away,
refusing to be found or ever accused.

No angel at the door guards our fate.
The breathing of this small and primitive human group
revolves on nothing more
than an early winter forest in the dark, borrowed
blankets and the convenience of cabin beds.

The parents are here and gone.
The children disperse like stars
in the debris of enormous stupidities,
faulted gestures, the persistent juvenalia
of bad will that is their inheritance.

Calm me. I cannot sleep.
I am the yellow pencil light,
from under the door of our own parents,
the violent question
in the nights that beg for dawn.

Wings of unloving brush my shoulders.
I have just begun to understand the unchanging
stone silence, the paradox of fixed weight
and untouchable pain, the unremovable
ambivalence in your walk or handhold
or goodbye smile.

Happiness on a Small Plate

I will take happiness on a small plate.
I will pretend it is not sucked
out of the air from a larger source
despite the faulty stem cells
or the damaged nerve endings
of the soul or the pained denying heart.
I could be cautiously well, if I
can practice forgetting
and hold the reality of you limited.

On that Rock

On that rock, on that fur,
a cry came and looped itself around us,
baleful lovers, otherwise so trapped.

I have this to report:
  I am alive in the land of the singing.

Birds at Night

I cannot leave this soft terrain, that
is my heart, that is my heart.
I feel the colors form again, the
hills to start, the hills to start.
Cry out bird! Japanese
arc of flight. I am
the space of the
golden screen. The
black on black of
crows at night
soft black on
black of birds
at night.

June 13, 1984

Ginny Stopped Dancing

Ginny stopped dancing years ago,
arms and legs agangle at the village hall,
to the stomp of country tunes and calls.
But not before she rammed her car
into a boulder in our circular drive, perhaps
the first sign of something amiss, her
misalignment with the world. She blamed
the boulder, an innocent quarter ton of granite.
Six months later her son, the meticulous
carpenter, lovingly fashioned her coffin
Shaker-style, plain as she was, and
chose the granite for the stone beneath which
she lies. Why did she die while I lived on?
I kept passing her cottage on the hill, pondering
this mystery. She twirled and leapt and
then the music within her went silent.
The fiddlers played on and others kept dancing.
Her son had a new sadness about him, his
workshop glowed bright with sunlight and quiet industry.
And I took life as it came.

Barbara McDougal

I know you Barbara McDougal going
in sanctimony to seven-fifteen Mass.
Who would believe that in those shoulders and
bent solemn head I see the spirit saying,
“Forgive, I forgive,” the spirit that pushes
evil and understanding aside, joyless.

Barbara orders her black heels custom from Carbone’s downtown,
the touch of vanity public in this just dawning
autumn day. She owns her mother’s five orientals
and from her Essex Street apartment she often wonders
where all the young coloreds come from and
if they are going to leave, for a war, for example.

In St. Mary’s this morning seven people stand
as the priest comes to the altar. His chasuble
sparkles, the hidden monstrance sparkles.
Barbara, you are sixty-eight. Are you tired?
Did you vote for the Kennedy boy?
Is the foam on the kneeler enough for your knees?
You would be repulsed by my arm on your stiff
shoulders. You always act as if nothing is happening.

Old Helen

Old Helen looking from her window rampart
Saw strawberries on the city sidewalk,
Soft and staining like blood from bodies wounded by love,
Or her father's cancerous cough, the dog dead of hemorrhage.
Running downstairs, dustpan and broom in hand
She found only a heap of rose petals as terrifying to her
As berries or blood. She swept the cement clean to purge
All illusion until, serene again, until dream-quiet
In her mind, with wild flying hair, she ascended
To her rooms of known disorder.

Leroy Street

The doll-house man wants you to know
that eighty percent of his customers
are adults over fifty who cannot be
bothered with the tiny wallpaper and rugs
but just want to buy the miniature furniture
for each precious room in these fully electric,
swivel-based, plexiglass-sided edifices
of glue, wax, wire, and hours of attention
to the minute details of domesticity.

Outside people are sleeping on the sidewalk.
Shirts jacked up to show bruises,
flies circling their crotches,
enormous in the taboo sphere each commands.
Once babies, now flesh in stupor, undone,
cradled in the depths of cardboard and rags,
newspaper and old coats.
Are they old, these totally vulnerable
public bodies who cannot be bothered or known
in their unknowing, unattended sleep?

The Poet and His New Love Appear at Dinner

"So how did you meet?" asks a bright-eyed bald man,
rocking forward on his toes to underscore
the prayerful importance of this question,
which she cannot answer with "None of your business"
because the poet's heart is everyone's business.
And he has been known to sit blankly,
features a composite of all the ordinary compromises
of love, stunned like a *cerf aux abois*,
in the living room, in the dining room,
too large to ignore, too familiar to abandon.
In such phases he won't dance; he talks
cobblestones of banality to them already footsore,
frightens their fatigued minds and his own
with news analysis, and wishes, as they all wish,
not to die without meaning.

. . .

We met in the lobby, we met in the bar,
we met in an elevator, going down.
Now, shining angels for the moment,
we give you our relief. In our hands
we hold you who guess that all truth
and all gentleness matter, nothing else.

White Dog Day

The white dog is sacrificed on the first cobalt
cloudless day in strawberry time, by Indian
men who never deceived with
"Here, boy, atta boy" or "Fetch, Samantha!"
the small packs of collarless mutts who
roam the reservation totally at home with
dirt roads and deer droppings, with the
loud late-night rides of teenagers and
Sam who fell asleep in
a meadow on a winter night and woke to
find his sister's dog curled hard against his back,
woke and walked to save his life, with the
dog trudging beside him, the same dog
he pointed out to me humping away under a cobalt
sky, nameless, and luckily brown and black,
not like the white puppy the children
told me confidently was next year's candidate,
while they nonchalantly tickled its belly

with their bare toes and played “Old Maid,”
under the one shade tree near a house for miles,
the same bitch belly that the dungareed men in heavy boots
would split in June or maybe July, without
malice, whose whiteness would become the
missing clouds, tossed up into the blue, whose
inside redness would soak into the strawberry roots
for the next year, whose many parts dumped
in the meadow would disperse like Orpheus
with bees and flies and birds and soaking rain
and deep snow unhindered
by words that could deceive and make
it want to stay, a restless soul
believing those strange sounds were more than
snore or giggle, more than today.

Squaw Valley, August 1986

When We Travel

When we travel
what we leave behind
is simply nothing
having ourselves
moving is all.

The Train

Tell me the train is coming
and that you'll be on it with
me, across Canada, through
the Rockies or down near
the Everglades. No matter where.

Lilacs

What I carried on the train
were lilacs, propped up and suffering
in a plastic glass, through Providence,
through Kingston and New Haven to you.

What I wanted was impossible,
new lilacs in heaps, new words.
Life-in-death, release, the presence
that bends over blindly.

If we two thieves are never happy again,
blame old gods who, though half-asleep,
noticed and were jealous when the sky
cleared briefly, when, all lies abandoned,
the grey river arched like a torso
and twisted brilliantly under Venus.

There are no new words; Piaf
on a carousel moans, *o mon amour*;
human sounds are exhausted to the
hiss of a laser.

Except in the mouths of lovers moving
close to sound's speed, turning to each other
with the almost-phrasing of
mute, perfect, branch-broken lilacs.

Woman on the Stairs

The woman with a tray of dishes
coming down the stairs, balanced against
the slippery wood risers, elbows out, knees bent,
is unwilling to fall or fly.
In the movies, the tray is dropped
when the uniformed maid sees the dead body.
Time after time, coffee cups crash to the floor
and some director shouts, "Cut!" In real life,
the rocking weight of cups and bowls,
the sickroom smell, the living soul in need
guide her balance one step
down to another. Once in a
while she wonders if it's time to
move the bed downstairs or call for help.

August 1986

August

The air on my ears is cold as if
I were driving too fast in a convertible,
at seventeen, down Route 3, with the
shameless highway roses shaking in cascades for miles.

Looking for enormous black wings in the August night,
I'm going to break through this and
break doing it. I'm going to take on August and
the way it kills the weak, its thunderstorms and exhaustions,
and play right into its arms. Every runt,
every sickly child, the fruit unfit for harvest
is mine, purloined from death.

I will copulate August back to the original travesty,
I will negotiate this rescue in the
dark, and sing in the heat of the cicada-drone *funerailles*
a counter-conspiracy into that silent,
unforgiving house, into the throats of my
almost-sleeping parents, soar over that roof
on black wings making the sound of every living dying thing.

Until these wings are translucent vibrations
all unborn, dissolved in the dying air of August.

August 1986

The Word as Sword

Emily Dickinson was right,
The word in print is a
Sword, a wound, a betrayal.
How am I to understand
This new intimacy of yours
Broadcast to the millions?
What have I become,
A woman alone,
While you write of sleeping
Or awake with another?
But I have joys wordless.
I concentrate on them.

With Time

With time, I am confident
these mysteries will erode
I will forget, become impervious
to the shock of pain and loss,
that you left for that new life.

Little Heart

With no false step and no hollow sound
Tess the dog says, “You go away so often
Today I am glad you are home
For my little heart is at peace.”

August 15, 1986

Esenin's Suicide

The great animal Sleep sits immobile on his chest,
Has kissed sweet pain into his face,
And shaped his mouth to the last word, "living."
Neck unbroken, he rode his soul to the golden stars.
I see what his eyes turned from.
I rub the cold forearms,
A child again in my arms.

September 4, 1986

The Ghost Hand

It can happen in a life.
You embrace one and
the hand you rest on the
shoulder blade is out in
the ghost world of the other, lost love.
The ideal shaped, the lost knowing
the ideal of myself.
If I lift my hand to that hand,
of course I die.

September

The flower's deepest part is a closed velvet whisper,
born enfolded on itself, sick perhaps one day to open
the little void to the wind, to sense the softening filaments,
the anther wings about to fall, the knot of blooming relaxing
to death. What is it? No sound really or the sound of
unknown-ness. Today the whisper is exhaled, unheard in a
velvet rush, over and over again at our feet, in this secret meadow.

My first vision came to life, that you were digging the ground
with your hands, showing me how.
Months later there were red potatoes
like jewels in the hay.

My second vision came to life, that you would lead me
to a table of strangers, on a farm,
in sunlight, then dusk.

My third vision has come
and gone, the serious couple
talking in a white waiting room.

This present silence has the weight of a weapon.

September 12, 1986

Shambling

A man at the grocery store, the last of
its kind, is polite and offers to
let me go ahead. But it isn't that.
It's his shambling manner, so like yours.
I turn away, not to be taken in again
by big awkward hands, by charming
diffidence, the sighs, the giant embrace.
He is hurt, I can tell. I would
like to say, look, it isn't you. It
was someone else, shambling.

Panis Angelica

There is a calm, I believe,
rising out of the well of misery,
but will it be enough?

Once my every cell was love-filled.
Once I was as translucent as
a holy wafer.

Some lovers leave brutally.
Others cut it fine with a knife.
The loyal sit in the front pews,
or the very last.

Angel bread
is become bread of men
on their tongues.

Borrego Springs

Outside the grocery store
two boys in a pickup display
two puppies. Says one boy,
they were dumped on the highway.
The grocery clerk, a teenage
girl, runs out to see them,
all four, and with her young
attention pats them in their
unextraordinary lostness.
What are the fates of these five
in the desert? At fifteen
the boys had the jobs of their
lives, in a truck
hauling something from the Salton Sea
to Encino, stopping at diners
where women still in blue jeans serve
the best coffee.

January 1987

The Diver's Tomb at Pæstum — Lockerbie 103

A boy dives from a cliff and
remains suspended and smiling. His
friends feast just below in fields of thyme
and sage where temples command the sea.
The ageless blue sky is his tomb.
We onlookers are above, are below, startled
at the long, high trajectory of his flight in stone.

Your letter promised you would return for the
holiday, but the plane burst apart and, victim
of hate, you were gone, sky blown.

Let me lift you, and Melissa, Robert,
Arthur, Elaine. What breaths I would
have held to change
your deaths. What corridors I would
have run down to block your way,
to unset time.

Poet

It's so useless for me to try to do
Other things. I am a poet.
It's like God. I've denied it.
And life has denied it for me.
But nothing, absolutely
Nothing changes my soul or
Alters my sensibility.

Cambridge, November 8, 1989

Zum Ghali

As far as I can tell, Zum Ghali
backed out of a Uccello canvas,
a modern horse. Now, stiff at attention
he pees majestically, retracts his penis
and, relaxed, begins the choreography
of the declension of his soul:

The horse autonomous, the horse alert,
the horse in lonely need, the horse
melancholic, the horse hungry, the
prideful steed, the dancing horse, horse
hesitant, horse beguiled.

Zum Ghali, I begin breathing where you
breathe behind the belly, hardly able
today to keep pace with your love,
weighed down with thoughts like
armored soldiers whose mouth
jerking and flank kicks
immobilize me; in the painting
I am this milk-white horse, heavy
and turning in frozen perspective.

I Love You

If there were world enough and time
I'd fashion you a better rhyme
But days are short
And time is fleeting
So you get an abbreviated Valentine greeting
    I love you
Days are short and time is money
I've barely time to tell you honey
If we dared to roll in fields of clover
Time's winged chariot would run us over
    Kiss me quick
We dared one time a long embrace
And lost three miles in life's short race.

All a Woman Wants

All a woman wants to hear is
I've loved you all my life
or something close to that.

Masters of Battle

For a short time we thought
Nothing of war — of hawks
Fled to the blue or of
Bravery, or of blood-soaked
France or the highlands
Of Vietnam or desert storms,
How brief, how careless we
Became, forgetting the
Masters of battle were
In dark conference,
Mapping boundaries of
Dread and unstoppable hate.

Left to play and
Dance, left to
Gentle love that
The masters — did they envy
The young — despised. We paid
For every minute we
Kept our eyes off them.
And into the future, the thoughtless
Well and living
Forget the dead or
Why they died.

The Only Woman

You're the only woman, he began
and faltered slightly, calculating
the scientific accuracy of this passionate
declaration, in whom I died and from whom
I emerged a phoenix. No, he resubmitted,
there was the girl, when I was in Paris,
twenty years ago. I told you. But
the point is that this sadness sits
like a crow on my shoulder. And
now we are both old and the denizens
of airports with no one to bid farewell
and no one to greet. Which is
why I called, he continued,
from that very phone booth
in that very transatlantic terminal
where we said goodbye, the only event of tenderness in
a public swirl of brutal motion, the pushing of
bodies and heft of luggage.

Franklin Park Zoo: Gorilla

A glare. An inch of glass between us.
Tempted I crouch, press my shoulder to yours.
Unbothered, you eat an apple, your nails
Brown and perfect, your eyes menacing
Like a Cardinal in chains.
The others stare disdainfully from
Artificial crags, dragging ropes and
Casually hurling tires.
Forgive me, my friends, my felons!

You turn your shoulder, disappear me.

Where was I once, forgetting the glass wall,
Startling someone on the other side?
A train or a waiting room, unaware and then this other,
Anxious, perhaps like you, at the sudden closeness,
These scentless human shadows on parade.

December 20, 2002

Believe

I believe everything
people say, that
the points connecting
a line bear time's
weight, that they have
not been playing, but
hard at work.
The roots of a tree
are lifting the bike path,
they crack the macadam
all day. Believe this,
the roots say. While
you slept, while you
listened to others, while
the river bore its moods
to the bay, these roots
did their slow work out
and up.

Night Planting / Impatient

This feeling for earth,
this touching of roots, just
after sundown, because
there was no time before,
insures the white roots a home
before black night.

This plant was rescued at 5:30
from the Woolworth's reduced rack
for a salvation no longer
than this summer, no longer
than my probing fingers trying
to fix the roots firm, sensitive
to the dirt of dirt, pressing down on
life to make life stay.

Pressing worms, shit, suspect little stones
that enmesh life in a city garden,
being pressed myself by darkness,
night laughs, diggings kind or ruthless
in time with some one or two's
sense of life, by spades chunk-chunking
somewhere, sometime for you or me.

Give me your hand and put it in the
earth here by mine, in the roots and
water, eager for the extraordinary night.

Spring Wind

The wind is blowing up a storm
but it's not a storm: The sky is
as blue as chicory blossoms, the
sun as bright as your eyes in the morning.
The trees with their new leaves
are bending against their will,
hoping for tomorrow's calm.
They've waited so long through the
winter frosts, with empty boughs,
song-less, until at last the
earth shifted and they could feel
the soil loosen around their roots.
For us, the windows are shaking,
but if you touch them they prove
warmed by sunshine.
Come, put your hand next to mine,
feel the hope of the high sun.
Hide with me today,
sheltered in the imaginary cottage
we dream of, by a never-changing
tropical sea. Tell the trees to be
patient. They need dance and
thrust for just a few more hours.
Like other storms, this one cannot
endure. Take it as a test
that brings strength.
What choice have we?

May 20, 2011

I Am Here for This Light

I am here for this light,
for the angle through the trees.
The sun is almost forgetting
its duty to set, behind
the thunder clouds.
I am here for early spring
green on old pines. The three
cedars guard the gate
as they have for six decades.
How grand this widening light
that knows its power is grown
disclaiming the night.
Who was seeking perfection?
The bay tide is flowing fast
behind the trees, unconscious.

How Our Summer House Speaks of Us

In the cabinets the spices we meant to use,
in bowls the chestnuts meant for rubbing
to ward off colds, the shelves of mismatched mugs.

Will our heirs forgive us if we die in
a plane crash, or slide off the road in
a blizzard, frozen before
our hearts cease beating?

Our summer house, Woods Hole, 1987–2018

Will they remember the
laughter, the children racing
up and down the stairs,
the guests who staggered
towards the kitchen, blind for coffee?
The young philosopher who
played clarinet in the barn,
the college girlfriends, boyfriends,
prospective spouses on bicycles?

Falmouth pink stones from the beach
scattered in the garden, in drawers,
in the grandchildren's sandy tin pails?

Julia, just four, woke from her nap
to her birthday party on the porch,
Jake turned cartwheels on the front lawn,
Sam in wonder blew soap bubbles
in the garden, baby Jesse
measured 28 inches on the kitchen wall,
and Claire, the youngest at farm camp,
wished for a pony.

Troves of souvenirs from
Russia, Greece, and China,
from relatives quiet now in albums.

At dusk, the pregnant deer gazing
confidently from the trees. The click
of the lock at night before
the coyotes yipped. Clean
sheets and deep sleep.

Will you know what we have lived
through to get this far? Does it matter?
Left in memory: A house of generosity,
of ease, leisure, and, yes, for that time,
no sadness or want.

Woods Hole, 2013

Prayer for M.

Even now, with the outlines of you barely clear
I wish you heart's ease, the soul quiet
of a window overlooking a small valley,
full of sky, you would be the untroubled climber
choosing points of rest and ascent.
Even now, I would keep you from harm,
move silently to stop an evil shadow,
weave in my mind a cloak of invisible light,
cast it about your undisturbed sleeping head
that you would wake in innocence.

In Saint Paul Church

Seeking refuge in cathedral half-light
after a deluge of tears,
under a siege of words,
I sat conjuring the certain storm without,
the clouds of fire bursting
in an ignorant sky,
trajectories of missiles
plowing undersea.
The ascendance of armaments
over the numerous innocents.
The weariness of soul
that breeds the energy of war.
And my thought was for you,
by gentle honesty protected.
Yet so mortal and so dear,
that I formed a prayer,
a child's plea,
a sister's loyalty,
a spouse's pledge,
a parent's protective cloak,
that the pity in the heart
would keep you safe.

Familiars

I am on the inside of your life.
When you go away, I know
where. Now in the changed light
you wipe your glasses, adjust
your bed pillows.
We are familiars.

Fingers

My fingers are twisted just like yours,
mother, grandmother, old man.
Was it some anger built up over the years
not twisted then, but twisting them now?

Things You Know

There will be things you know
I couldn't guess,
mysteries in me that you would break
apart as easily as a child
drops a glass and is surprised
it shatters. Pain for me,
for you a diagnosis so obvious
you see no question, just
the law immutable, relentless.
Sleep on while
I keep watch for us both.

Mortality

I never thought mortality
would catch us both. You were
so golden, without hesitancy, and
now, unrelaxed and practiced,
you perform anywhere with the same
disdainful ease. And so do I,
but never without thinking you were
the only one. I had hoped,
before this age had me in its hold,
to soar, a breakaway spirit, an innocent.

Matthew and Jeanne, Cambridge, 2018

Jeanne at home, 2018

If I Were Going to Stay

If I were going to stay
I'd buy the biggest
bouquet of flowers
for the table in the window.

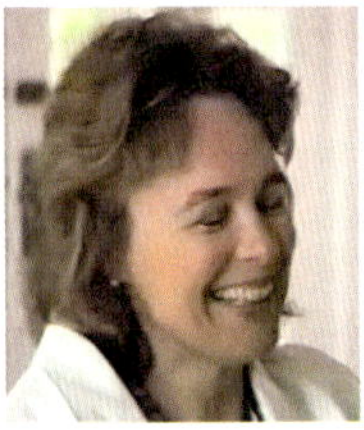

Grace was in all her steps . . . In every gesture, dignity and love.
— John Milton

Jeanne Guillemin-Meselson was born March 6, 1943 in Brooklyn, NY, to James and Eileen Harley Garrigan, the second of five children. In 1952, the family moved to Rutherford and then to Upper Montclair, New Jersey, where she attended Lacordaire Academy, a Dominican college preparatory school. In 1962 she went to Paris, attending classes at the École des Beaux-Arts and the Sorbonne. There she married Robert Guillemin, an American painter with whom, in 1964, she had twin boys, Rob and John. Returning to the United States later that year, she attended Harvard College (A.B. 1968, social psychology) and Brandeis University (Ph.D. 1973, sociology and anthropology, with field work in Antigua). She was appointed Instructor in Sociology at Boston College in 1972, soon becoming Professor of Sociology, teaching anthropology and

sociology. She divorced Robert Guillemin in 1979 and in 1986 married Harvard University biologist Matthew Meselson, legally changing her surname to Guillemin-Meselson in 2011. In 2005, Jeanne left Boston College in order to have more time for writing, becoming Senior Advisor in the Security Studies Program at the MIT Center for International Studies where she conducted research, guided graduate students and established an endowed fund that provides financial support to women studying for the doctoral degree in international affairs. Jeanne was a Radcliffe Institute Fellow (1972–73), a Congressional Fellow of the American Anthropological Association, serving on the Senate Finance Committee staff (1978–79), and a Research Fellow at the Hastings Center for the Study of Society, Ethics and the Life Sciences (1980–81). She served on the boards of the American Folklife Center of the Library of Congress (1982–87); Transaction Books (1996–2012); the Human Rights Review (1999–2002); and Society/Transaction (1988–1997). She was a member of the World Economic Forum Global Agenda Council on Nuclear, Biological and Chemical Weapons (2011–16), regularly attending its meetings in Dubai. Jeanne left three novels at various stages of completion: *Zoo Berlin*, *Freud's Sisters* and *My Brooklyn*. Her six published books are *Urban Renegades: The Cultural Strategy of American Indians* (Columbia University Press, 1975); *Mixed Blessings: Intensive Care for Newborns*, with Lynda Holmstrom (Oxford University Press, 1986); *Anthrax: The Investigation of a Deadly Outbreak* (University of California Press, 1999); *Biological Weapons: From the Invention of State-Sponsored Programs to Contemporary Bioterrorism* (Columbia University Press, 2004); *American Anthrax: Fear, Crime, and the Investigation of the Nation's Deadliest Bioterrorist Attack* (Times/Holt, 2011). Her last book, *Hidden Atrocities: Japanese Germ Warfare and American Obstruction of Justice at the Tokyo Trial* (Columbia University Press, 2017), was nominated for a Pulitzer Prize, the Robert Merton Award, and the Lemkin Award.

Jeanne, Athens, 2016

Acknowledgments

Cynthia Linkas, Patricia Lorsch, Betsy Seifter, and Miriam Weinstein, the four other members of Jeanne's writing group, gave many loving hours to the discussion and initial selection of the poems. When it became evident that creation of a book was more than we could manage by ourselves, they suggested that I turn to freelance editor Sally Brady and book designer Bruce Kennett to bring the book into existence. Their outstanding talents are evident in this volume. For her help in many ways, I am indebted to Darline Desronville, Jeanne's confidante and helper in Jeanne's last months. Thanks to Jen and Rob Guillemin for their thoughtful contributions, and to John Guillemin for his portrait of Jeanne. Throughout the whole time, Janet Montgomery kept everything in good order and on schedule.

If I Were Going to Stay is one of the first books to be composed in Goluska, a new typeface from lettering artist Rod McDonald, Canada's foremost designer of printing types. McDonald named his latest design in honor of his longtime friend Glenn Goluska, who was for decades a mainstay in Toronto's letterpress printing scene, and who delighted in printing books of poetry. McDonald also cites the Boston type designer and artist W. A. Dwiggins as an inspiration for his design. Goluska is destined to become a classic for use in the composition of beautiful books.

Penmor Lithographers printed the book on acid-free Mohawk Superfine paper; Superior Finishing provided the binding, using traditional Smythsewn construction and all-cotton Cialinen cloth woven in Italy. Bruce Kennett planned the design and typography, with assistance from Sally Brady and Matthew Meselson.